The Magic of DARTMOOR

DAVID MUDD

BOSSINEY BOOKS

First published in 1994 by Bossiney Books,
St Teath, Bodmin, Cornwall.
Typeset and printed by Penwell Ltd, Callington, Cornwall.

ISBN 0 948158 96 4

ACKNOWLEDGEMENTS

Front cover: Roy Westlake
Front cover design: Maggie Ginger
Modern photographs: Ray Bishop; Diana Mudd

AUTHOR'S ACKNOWLEDGEMENTS

*THE author would like to thank his publisher, Michael Williams, for his
encouragement and support throughout an association celebrating its 21st
anniversary in 1994.*

*He is grateful, too, for the editorial skills of Angela Larcombe; the pho-
tography of his wife, Diana, and that of Ray Bishop, and thanks as well,
Alan Endacott (of the Museum of Dartmoor Life) and David German (of
Princetown) for their help in suggesting and lending old prints and illus-
trations for this book.*

About the Author

AFTER *thirteen solo books and five collaborations with other writers on aspects of life, crime, history and industry in his native Cornwall, David Mudd literally crossed the Tamar in 1992 to live, with his wife Diana, just inside the Dartmoor National Park.*

The former journalist, radio and television personality (as well as Member of Parliament for Falmouth and Camborne from 1970 to 1992) celebrated by writing the well-acclaimed **Dartmoor Reflections**, *published in October 1993 by Bossiney Books.*

Before that book had even appeared in the shops of Dartmoor, he was at work on this companion volume, **The Magic of Dartmoor.**

The Magic of Dartmoor

DESPITE its granite ruggedness, Dartmoor has a great deal in common with a huge sheet of tissue-paper. Spread it flat and it is dull, obvious and featureless. But crumple it and then peer into the many folds, wrinkles, creases and unseen places of concealment and revelation and magic are but a hair's breadth away.

Look down on Dartmoor from an aircraft, or across it from a tor – what can be seen, although fascinating, may hardly justify a second look. Yet walk across it and gaze into its gulfs, its crannies, its quiet villages, its dark and brooding woods and copses, its bracken and its rivers ... and it rapidly changes from a mere geographical feature to a rich cauldron in which the unexpected – often the unbelievable – simmers and erupts in a weird turbulence that brings together the inexplicable and, at times, the echoes of a dark past.

It's a past that does not always accept the present, let alone come to grips with the future!

A few years ago when, with a waving of flags and the sound of trumpets, electricity finally came to an isolated hamlet, a journalist asked one of those who was to benefit just how she would gain from the march of progress.

Hardly pausing to think, she ventured that the electric light would certainly make it easier to see to trim the wick of her oil lamps in future ...

William Crossing, a century earlier, found the same reluctance to encompass the new with any degree of confident enthusiasm. He discovered a man who disdained the 'new-fangled matches' and continued to rely on his trusted method of lighting his pipe. Wrote Crossing: '*We never heard him deride modern usages, but we*

GRIMSPOUND ... A primitive stronghold high on Dartmoor.

noticed he refrained from adopting them. Though a smoker, he used no matches, always carrying with him a flint and steel and a piece of rag which had been steeped in a solution of saltpetre for tinder. He dispensed altogether with the box, and we have seen him obtain a light for his pipe by wrapping the rag around his finger and dextrously dropping the spark on it. The flints he used were probably the flakes or scrapers of a bygone age, which, as he informed us, he used to pick up on the Moor.'

Another Moorman known to Crossing was reluctant even to venture into the seething metropolis of Princetown. When a visit was unavoidable, he conducted his business as quickly as possible before making a speedy exit.

Then there is the boding evil of some of the names – Wistmans Wood, Gibbet Hill, Grimspound, Devil's Bridge and the like.

Wistmans Wood is believed to date back to the days of the druids and to have supernatural influences working within it. Indeed, although the records suggest that when its heart was eaten out by fire in 1882, the cause was the carelessness of casual visitors failing to extinguish a fire after a picnic, there are those who recall that those suspected of the outbreak were later traced and cleared of accidental incendiarism.

There are some, therefore, who believed that unmentionable dark forces came into play.

Gibbet Hill, between Mary Tavy and Lydford, has an equally unappealing reputation in that it is claimed that its high prominence over the surrounding countryside made it the ideal place for criminals to be hung high there in iron cages and left until, eventually, their whitened bones dropped through the bars of their personal prison.

It is doubtful if the friends of one felon actually did him a favour by prolonging his life in an ingenious way. Forbidden to give him food, they took him a supply of candles which he gradually ate.

LYDFORD CHURCH ... The Watchmaker's Tomb lies in the shadow of the village church walls.

Is the black reputation of Gibbet Hill yet another piece of 'created' Dartmoor magic? Perhaps there is a strong pointer in that one of the gateways leading to it is still known as Ironcage Gate.

Grimspound probably takes its name from the Anglo-Saxon word for the Evil One – 'Grima'. Although, like all the other pounds of Dartmoor, its main function was to provide a protection for cattle, Grimspound was undoubtedly designed as a fortification to which, in the days of Caesar, it would have been usual for people to flee as the Roman army passed by. It was described by the Rev Samuel Rowe as: *'this remarkable specimen of a primitive town, fortified by a strong wall, and containing numerous remains of ancient dwellings within its cyclopean bulwark'*.

Then there's the magic of the Dartmoor craftsman. He was often self-educated yet, without the benefits of schooling or even rudimentary equipment, could reach the most advanced levels of skill. One such man is glowingly remembered by a tomb in the shelter of the porch at Lydford church. In a masterpiece of puns and allusions, his life and achievements are perpetuated in these immortal words: *'Here lies, in horizontal position, the outside case of George Routleigh, watchmaker, whose abilities in that line were an honour to his profession; integrity was the mainspring and prudence the regulator of all the actions of his life; humane, generous and liberal, and his hand never stopped till he had relieved distress; so nicely regulated were all his movements that he never went wrong except when set agoing by people who did not know his key; even then he was easily set right again! He had the art of disposing his time so well that the hours glided away in one continual round of pleasure and delight, till an unlucky moment put a period to his existence! He departed this life, November 14, 1802, aged 57. Wound up in hopes of being taken in hand by his Maker, and being thoroughly cleansed, repaired, and again set agoing in the world to come'.*

What a pity it is that there was nobody available to pay a similar tribute to the mason who wrote, and inscribed, so glowing a testimonial to a fellow being!

The years that lie ahead might indeed end the joys of the magic of Dartmoor that can be seen and enjoyed by present generations of lovers and visitors.

Will the magic of isolation be removed as personal transport spurts ahead?

Will the magic of a ghostly past be laid to rest by some bright scientist who proves – conclusively – that the unexplained cannot exist?

Will the magic of the mellow mists and rich colour-tones created by the vagaries of nature be over-ruled by those who will one day control the elements?

And what of the wild-life?

The pine-marten, the pole-cat, the wild-cat all have been extinguished from Dartmoor by the insensitivity of man.

And what of the badger? Could Brock, the last of the bear family to be found in Britain, face extinction at the hands of scientists and experts who believe that he poses a threat to the welfare and health of cattle?

If so, then will Badger's Holt – that delightful place of refresh-

TODAY … Badger's Holt is a tourist attraction. Below: as it was.

ment so conveniently situated just beside Dartmeet – become a name inspiring the question from tomorrow's children: 'Mummy, what was a badger?'

'Oh, no', say the wise and the knowing – as they have said so many times before – 'things *never* change on Dartmoor.'

But they do! But the way memories are also kept so vibrantly alive despite time, doubt and disbelief is the *real* magic of Dartmoor.

The White Rajah, the Refugee Squire ... and the Sea-dog who Founded a Water-supply

F orget your water-diviners with their leaping twigs; heed not the well-borers; put not your faith in aquatic engineers. If abundant supplies of water are needed in even the longest and most severe times of drought and shortage, call upon the spirit of Sir Francis Drake.

For it was he who found the secret of undiminished supplies of clear, fresh water on Dartmoor.

Whilst galloping his horse down from the heights of Dartmoor, he found that the water followed hard on his heels. So hard, in fact, that it was sufficient both in flow and in quality to create an adequate supply for the area centred on Plymouth.

Although the story is rather fanciful, it is true that Drake was – during occasional off-moments from his ships and men – involved in organising a water supply from Dartmoor to the city. In 1589, the corporation of Plymouth gave him £800 to create a link between the River Meavy and Plymouth. He was allowed to keep £200 for himself, but instructed to use the balance to purchase access-rights from landowners holding properties along the route.

There was nothing particularly ingenious in the scheme as Plymouth and Devonport had long been served by the waters of dozens of Dartmoor streams. What was of interest, however, was the scale of the operation; the speed with which it was created; and the way in which – in turn – it led to one of Dartmoor's most spectacular man-made features, Burrator reservoir.

Work started in December 1590 and, by the end of April 1591, a 25-mile system was in place and operating.

Others improved on his concept and the chosen route and, by the late 1800s, Drake's leat from Meavy joined the century-old supplies

11

PRECIOUS RESOURCE ... Water cascades into Burrator Reservoir.

drawn from the Blackabrook, Cowsic and West Dart rivers to be impounded in the vast reservoir built by Plymouth corporation and completed in 1898.

Work had taken some seven years to complete, including the laying of rows of 6-ton granite blocks, each of them quarried and dressed on site. The intention was that, with a surface area of 150 acres, it could hold over 600 million gallons of water. This target was eventually reached and, in 1928, its size was increased from its original capacity to one billion gallons.

Sir Francis is still remembered with affection and gratitude, annually, some four hundred years after he first guaranteed water to Plymouth. At the modern reservoir, some one-and-a-half miles long, more than half-a-mile wide, and twenty-five metres deep at its deepest point, dignitaries still gather for the annual Fyshinge Feaste. They solemnly – but appropriately – drink two toasts in pure water.

The first is to Sir Francis himself, but the second is more interesting: 'may the descendants of him who brought us water never want wine'. The 'descendants' bit is particularly apt as he died leaving no sons. The title passed to his nephew who was created a baronet in 1662.

There was something rather appropriate in that, of the various rivers and watercourses open to him in seeking water for Plymouth, Sir Francis was attracted to the river Meavy.

Meavy's name is taken from 'mew', an old word for the cry of sea-birds.

When Drake was but a young man, one feature of the Meavy landscape was already well over three hundred years old – the famous Meavy oak. Although it's impossible to date it with any degree of accuracy, local belief is that it goes back to the early days of the thirteenth century. Not in dispute is its immense girth and the claim that it is so vast that nine people once dined inside its hollow trunk.

Drake's waterworks, by the way, were once described as being 'the greatest example of engineering skill of the sixteenth century'. Certainly the scheme suggested a down-to-earth dedication that

VILLAGE CENTRE ... The bridge at Horrabridge is a focal point of the village.

13

PEACEFUL SCENE ... Sheepstor Church.

was repeated earlier this century when the future of Meavy school was threatened because of falling numbers.

Refusing to accept defeat, the local vicar approached the lord of the manor and obtained a parcel of land. Using funds carefully raised and earmarked for a village hall, a band of volunteers bought necessary materials and gave their own time and skill to build a school to be owned, maintained and used by Meavy's children. And, to remind everyone of the indomitable spirit of those committed to the venture, it was agreed that instead of a bell being rung for morning assembly, the summons would come from the beating of a drum!

Had Meavy lost its school, then youngsters would have had to go to Walkhampton where, coincidentally, they would have found a similar spirit of commitment in the shape of a Free School founded in 1719 by Elizabeth Modyford.

Determined that the village children should have a strong religious and well-based education, she paid for the school and endowed it with the annual proceeds from 162 acres of land.

This was farmed and managed so efficiently that the annual value of the endowment reached over £1000 and was enough to maintain

14

the school; employ two teachers; provide forty free places; and make clothing available for poor pupils.

Walkhampton stands but a stone's throw away from the river Walkham, the valley in which it lies dating back to the Bronze Age. Nearby is Horrabridge, its name a corruption of 'Horebridge' (boundary bridge) marking the coming-together of the parishes of Walkhampton, Sampford Spiney and Whitchurch.

Sampford Spiney boasts an unbelievable number of ancient farmhouses, with the distinguished Devon historian, Dr W G Hoskins, selecting Warne's Kitchen as: *'one of the best examples to be found of the old Dartmoor farmhouse in which there was direct communication between the living-room and the cattle-shippen'*. He estimates it dates from the early 1500s.

Sampford Spiney is also famous for its remote and rugged setting, it being claimed that it was created when the Devil's apron broke and let fall an avalanche of huge granite boulders he happened to be carrying at the time.

The confusing part about Dartmoor names is that they sound so convincing that it is assumed that they mean what they say or

FAMILY SEAT ... The ruins of Longstone Manor, home of the Elfords.

sound.

We've already met Horrabridge (boundary bridge), and Meavy (from 'cry of the sea birds'). Yelverton comes from 'Ella's Ford', which – in turn – is a corruption of 'elder-tree ford'. So, can Sheepstor be as obvious as it seems? After all, it is populated by legions of grazing sheep.

No, the name comes from a Celtic word – 'Syth', meaning 'steep' and certainly not 'sheep'. But, then again, it isn't particularly steep, either. Its name also occurs as 'Shitestor' or 'Shittor'.

Being positive, though, there are enough riddles concerning Sheepstor without bothering about its name.

Where, for instance, did Squire Elford hide? Why shouldn't we copy him? Why is the red granite of Aberdeen found amidst the grey granite of Dartmoor? What is the Sheepstor link with an outpost of China Seas piracy?

The Elford family, lords of the manor of Longstone, were pretty frightened folk during the Civil War. Fearful of arrest, Squire Elford popped off to the local pixies' cave and, in a narrow chamber some two metres by one-and-a-half, took effective refuge from Cromwell's men.

To help pass the time, he painted pictures on the walls.

However, the Dartmoor historian and vicar of Crediton, the Rev Samuel Rowe, warned – in the mid-1800s – against going to what he called the 'Pisky House' where the squire hid. *'The opening is exceedingly difficult to find without a guide,'* he wrote.

'It is under an overhanging mass of moorstone. The passage proceeds at first in a straight direction, but suddenly turns and terminates in a sort of recess, where two or three persons might lie concealed. The notion that this cave is the resort of the piskies or pixies appears still to be extant in the neighbourhood'.

So, if you don't like piskies, then don't follow the path to Squire Elford's refuge!

John Elford, by the way, probably needed a refuge in that he married four times. One of his wives was buried at Widecombe, and another with him at Sheepstor where he is commemorated by a memorial in the south porch of the church bearing the initials 'JE' and the year 1640.

As, however, the Civil War lasted from 1642 until 1649, either the

MOORSTONE … Overhanging rocks can hide secrets.

JE was another person altogether; or John Elford didn't hide from Cromwell's men; or he'd been dead for several years before his legendary cultural incarceration in the 'Pisky House'.

But does it really matter?

The facts about the red Aberdeen granite being brought to Dartmoor are beyond cynical speculation.

James Brooke, who lived from 1803-1868, was born at Benares, in India, and educated at Norwich. When he was 35, he sailed from London to Sarawak with the task of eliminating the piracy that was rife on the north-west coast of Borneo. He had the necessary military background, having served in the private army of the East India Company, and having been wounded in 1826.

He was so successful in flushing out the pirates that he was made Rajah of Sarawak – 'the White Rajah' – in 1841, by order of the Sultan of Borneo.

Not wishing to rest on his laurels, he then led a campaign against rebel tribes; masterminded free trade; drew up a new penal code;

and outlawed the traditional head-hunting habits of the Dyak tribesmen by making head-taking a head-losing offence.

His attempts to stamp-out opium-smuggling meant his having to lead a native army against Chinese irregulars. Again, he succeeded.

He was rewarded by the British government with a knighthood, in 1847, and the governorship of Labuan.

In 1858 he retired to Devon and bought an estate at Burrator where he remained until his death in 1868, the line of 'White Rajahs' being continued through his nephew and his great-nephew.

Although Sir James loved Dartmoor, there has never been any real explanation for the decision that his grave should be marked with a gigantic tomb of red granite from Aberdeen.

RESTING PLACE ... Rajah Brook's grave.

18

The Lights, the Hounds, the Witch and the Hare

INSIGNIFICANT words used with disarming innocence often turn out to have an unexpected richness of meaning.

Look at those, for instance, of the writer Arthur H Norway. With the air of someone mentioning the quality of Devonshire cooking in the most general of terms, thus missing the individual textures and tastes of its many dishes, he wrote of 'this land of ancient superstition'.

How rich a land – and how ancient and varied.

Dartmoor is indeed a land of fable; of superstition; of horror and of the unbelievable ... a land of legend where only the foolish or the ignorant would dare to be arrogantly adamant in their rejection of the unexplained or the unexperienced.

For it could all have happened; actually be happening today; or, possibly, waiting in the wings and happening tomorrow.

Take Jack o'Lantern, for instance.

Know-alls might scoff and say that, after a hot and dry summer, vegetation decaying in a bog can give off methane gas which, as it bubbles through the mire, ignites and creates a myriad of dancing blue flashes.

But are they right? How did methane gas save a man from a lonely, lost fate? How does methane gas know where a death is about to take place? And how could a clergyman not have known the difference between gas and a spectral being?

Yet, no less an authority than the Rev Sabine Baring-Gould whilst walking near Yelverton, saw: *'a little blue flame dancing on a pool. I went on my knees and went close to it to make sure what it was, and that it was not a glow-worm'.*

No mention, there, of methane.

WOODS AND WATER … The Dartmoor landscape conceals the unexplained and the mysterious.

The words of another nocturnal walker near Huccaby bridge: *'They appeared like the flash of a lantern, disappeared and then presently appeared again … From a distance, the light appeared to be considerable but – on approach – appeared only as a small greenish-blue flame about three feet (one metre) above the soil'.*

Was it Jack o'Lantern who was seen dancing above the stacked corn where the sickly son of a Dartmoor farmer broke a blood vessel and dropped dead?

Could it be methane, and not Jack o'Lantern that is seen leaving a churchyard before travelling down the lanes and waiting outside the door of a sick person, awaiting the emergence of a second flame from inside at the moment of death?

And was it methane, rather than Jack o'Lantern that responded to the prayer of a farm-worker lost overnight in a lonely part of Dartmoor?

Judge for yourself.

He was lost and, being God-fearing, prayed for a guide. *'All at once a little light sprang up and moved forward. He knew that it was Jack o'Lantern and that it was held to lead into dangerous places; but his confidence in Providence was so strong: and so assured was he that the light was sent in answer to his prayer that he followed it. He was conducted over ground fairly firm tho' miry till he reached heather and a sound footing, whereupon the flame vanished'.*

Would be methane be as helpful?

What of the Hound of the Baskervilles? In days when it is accepted that 'big cats' stalk the hedges of Dartmoor, can anyone seriously doubt that Conan Doyle's huge black hound does not still live in the secret cracks and crevices around Hound Tor, emerging at night to feast on cattle and to terrorise those who undoubtedly *do* see it but who are reluctant to admit what they know to be a fact?

Polluted as it is by environmental noise, the modern ear may be unable to identify a cracking whip and a strange baying in the midst of a relentless and vicious gale sweeping across the Moor and down through Wistman's Wood. But to the unsophisticated and unpolluted hearing organ, there is no mistaking the sounds of the Wish Huntsman, urging his baying hounds to greater effort in their endless search, pushed ever onwards by the relentless cracking of his whip.

As William Crossing wrote in the last century – and what was true then cannot be less so now: *'Much that the Dartmoor peasant now regards with scepticism was not so very long since most implicitly believed in by him. But though the hold that superstition once had upon him is gradually getting less firm, it has by no means entirely relinquished its grasp. He will talk about "wistness" by which he means a sepulchral appearance, and though usually confessing that he himself has never encountered such, can hardly be persuaded that what he has heard about others having done so is not true.'*

Crossing, of course, was right. Because a person has not actually experienced something for himself does not eliminate its reality or its presence.

How many people saw Childe, the hunter, perish in the way told?

Yet his tomb exists; so why go to the bother of building a solid tomb if the story might seem a little flimsy?

After all, certain people may have had a vested interest in discrediting what really happened that cold night so many years ago when, facing death in a blizzard, he slew his horse and used its warm corpse as a coat. As even that lost its warmth, he wrote his will in blood on some convenient nearby stones, leaving his land and his possessions to whoever should find him.

It seems that the monks of Tavistock found the body and, as it was at a place outside their jurisdiction, carted the corpse to their own abbey so they could claim his fortune.

It surely stands to reason, therefore, that the worthy clerics had a definite interest in trying to kid successive generations that it was all a bit of rural superstition.

How better to disguise your own mischief by discrediting the true source of your immoral gain!

Disparaged, too, are the exploits of Sir John Fitz, of Tavistock, and his very unpleasant daughter Lady Howard. After all, any town acquiring Elizabethan respectability would try to cast a discreet veil over that which local people believed to be true.

By the time Lady Howard (charmingly described three hundred years later as 'that grim old woman') was old enough to embark upon her lifetime's attainment of marrying and outliving a couple of brace of wealthy worthies, her dad was setting what was to become the impeccable family hallmark of murder and mayhem.

Sir John began life as a disappointment to his parents.

As the best of Tavistock's soothsayers had warned that he was going to be a nasty bit of work, his proud parents called in medical aid to try to induce premature birth so that he would be born under a more favourable umbrella of astrology. But despite the ministrations of the medics, their pills, potions, oils, incantations and hot baths, he stayed firm in his mother's womb and eventually emerged on the wrong side of the cusp.

He grew up, it is said: *'to be a turbulent, dangerous man, very dangerous with his sword on all occasions'*. In all fairness, he never lost an argument – merely by using the playful habit of spearing any adversaries with steel blade before being out-talked.

Clearly fearing the local council might object to having to undertake a weekly collection of bodies from his back door, he would take the corpses – at the dead of night – and lay them by the roadside to suggest they were the innocent victims of brutal highway robbery.

CHILDE'S TOMB ... The memorial to a hunter who perished on the moor.

Sadly, before claiming what would have been his rightful place in the Elizabethan Book of Unmentionable Records, he went into so advanced and progressive a state of depression, melancholia and remorse that – arguing with himself one night – he applied his usual custom for ending an argument and stabbed himself to death.

The loss of her father clearly gave his daughter, Lady Howard, a split personality. According to some records she was good and gracious. She was, it was said, a woman of great force of character – a

23

A GHOSTLY COACH … The spectral vehicle used by Lady Howard on her nightly journey from Tavistock to Okehampton Castle.

saintly person – who befriended all and opposed the greed of her husbands.

Her enemies, on the other hand, portrayed her as an atrocious monster who overcame obstacles – especially husbands – by mortal elimination. Be that as it may, she was certainly oft-widowed. Being a practical sort of person, she recycled the bones of her departed spouses and used them to make a ghostly coach in which she enjoyed a spectral nightly burn-up, the four corners of her Deathmobile being decorated with the four skulls.

As an (anonymous) poet put it:
'My lady's coach hath nodding plumes;
the driver hath no head;
My lady is an ashen white,
like one that is long dead.'

Small wonder that few people, nowadays, don't admit to encountering the ghost of Lady Howard ... but how many do see her, but keep quiet about it?

Should we not be told?

And why, too, should history forget the ingenuity of a gifted Dartmoor woman who turned witchcraft to gain in a sporting way?

Dabbling with her cauldron, she found she could turn herself into a hare at will. Chatting with her grandson, she learned that one of the local gentry was so hooked on hunting that he would pay sixpence ($2\frac{1}{2}$p) to anyone telling him where a hare could be found.

Witch and grandson struck-up a partnership. He would tell and she would run. They would pocket the money and, by outracing the hounds, she would escape unscathed.

Eventually, it seems, the hunter smelled a rat and suspected that if the woman were *not* a witch, there must be some other reason why the hunted hare always disappeared into her cottage as the exhausted hounds fell further and further behind.

Determined to put his theory to the test, he concealed a second set of hounds near her cottage. As the escaping hare meandered past, he released them.

In hot pursuit, dogs, hunter and parson burst into the woman's bedroom and found her in bed, gasping for breath. Although she had changed herself back into human form, her body bore the wounds of many dog-bites.

She was accused, convicted of witchcraft and sentenced to death by burning. At the pyre she recanted and was reprieved.

Soon, however, she was back doing her successful transformation act and had, eventually, to meet her death at the stake.

Lest there be those who would dismiss a ghostly presence on the grounds that it was many years ago, let them ponder on this. As recently as the 1920s a new phenomenon entered the currency of Dartmoor supernatural when, it was said, a pair of Hairy Hands, caused accidents on the stretch of road approaching Postbridge from Two Bridges.

The hands, it was said, appeared from nowhere and – ending at the wrist – still had the strength to over-ride the corrective actions of mortal drivers and turn vehicles off the road and either onto the verge or, in some cases, to overturn them entirely.

MOORLAND ROAD … Peaceful by day – but at night can it be peopled by ghostly coaches – or hairy hands that take over the wheel?

The Admiral and the College

Ignore the obvious temptation to call the picture overleaf 'where sheep may safely graze'; disregard the splendid cricket pavilion looking for all the world like an item of scenery awaiting the arrival of the principals for the balcony scene in Romeo and Juliet; be blind to the splendid buildings of Kelly College, in the 1920s, and the caption becomes obvious.

From the south of the straw-boatered, plus-foured gent holding his pants up in the foreground comes an immense and imaginary 'word bubble' as he asks the immortal words: 'Has anybody here seen Kelly?'

For indeed many of those to have passed through the portals of the great college on the outskirts of Tavistock have never heard of Kelly, let alone seen him.

Benedictus Marwood Kelly was born at Holsworthy on February 3, 1785. He was buried there on October 26 1867, some ten years before the college that was to bear his name opened its doors to its first batch of pupils in September 1877.

At the age of twelve – as was by no means unusual in those days – he entered the Royal Navy. He did not enlist, however, in the 'boy officer' rank of Midshipman, but as an Able Seaman, described by an Admiral of the time as being 'the lowest form of animal life in the Navy'.

Despite the dangerous and demanding life which made longevity a rarity amongst seafarers, he climbed the career ladder and in 1821 was promoted to the rank of Captain and put in command of *HMS Royal George*. It was one of the rare periods when Britain was not actually officially at war with anyone, and his task was to sail the seas off the coasts of Africa to intercept and capture ships car-

rying slaves, whatever their nationality.

In this theatre of operations he picked up a severe intestinal complaint that crippled him both physically as well as mentally. He knew that something was amiss, but could not find a doctor who could lay a finger on what was wrong and dispense sympathy and understanding as well as medicine. This created a major nervous debility which increased in its severity with each doctor he saw.

One surgeon, in Madeira in 1829, merely suggested he should *try the Waters of the Baths of Gurnigal*. Another gave him *some mercurial ointment to rub upon my legs. I was so weak I could barely stand*, he wrote, *but I continued this treatment for this two months. It did me great harm, I believe the fellow's object was to make a job of me*.

Invalided out of active service, he was one of the first officers to be accorded reserve status when it was introduced by Queen Victoria in the early 1850s and assumed the commission of Vice-Admiral, progressing to full Admiral in April of 1863, by which time he was already over seventy-eight years of age.

Victoria was very kind to veterans!

Married for the first time, in 1837, his wife died about one year later. Friends and associates who visited him were quite taken aback by what they saw.

As a director of two major railway companies and of the Royal Mail Packet Service, he should have lived comfortably. They found Kelly, however, living in a manner *that was so economical as to be called penurious. He had no home and but one room to sleep in. Friends and relations undertook all his washing and mending*, it was noted.

Where had his wealth gone, people wondered.

The answer would only emerge some thirty years later. Kelly was noted as an outspoken man who, although fully aware of the weaknesses in even the strongest of human nature, always sought out the good. He did not tolerate incompetence or inefficiency. Brusque and businesslike, he was kind and considerate as well. Additionally, based on his period in the Royal Navy, he felt that whilst the children of Army officers were generally well cared-for, the education accorded the offspring of those afloat left much to be desired.

Although life at sea kept him away from Devon for years at a time, he was as much a patriotic ambassador for his home county as he was a loyal officer and servant of the Crown.

Of Windsor castle he wrote: *'This castle is worthy of being tenanted by monarchs reigning over the most powerful of nations'*.

Looking at a famous waterfall in Austria, he observed cuttingly that it *'has not half the picturesque beauty of the Lydford cataract in my own dear county'*. Viewing the coast of France he observed: *'Rob it of its delightful climate and its magnificent Alps as a background, and I have seen scenery more beautiful in my own dear Devonshire'*.

And the whereabouts of his suspected fortune?

On September 29 1867, three days after his death, his Will was read. It told all.

Kelly directed that, in accordance with his beliefs, he wished to see created a centre of educational excellence to be named after him. He had scrimped, saved and invested to amass the breathtaking sum of £132,000 with which to build and endow a college.

Geographically he did not actually select Tavistock. He merely directed that his Trustees should *'hire, or otherwise procure, a suitable school house to be situated in the county of Devon on the west side of a line drawn north and south through the parish church of the town of North Tawton, in the said county'*.

Tavistock was finalised as the site when, in 1874, the eighth Duke of Bedford presented twenty acres to the east of the town for Kelly's college to be built.

Conditional on the money being paid from Kelly's estate was the blueprint that the college should be conducted 'in accordance with the principles of the Church of England as by law established'. The curriculum, he had instructed, was *'not to be classical only, but may include foreign languages, science and literature'*.

With the money guaranteed and the land donated, work began.

Kelly College welcomed its first intake of scholars in September 1877, but within a decade was facing up to the need for enlargement that was to become a fact of success for many years to come.

The first headmaster, Robert West Taylor (1877-1885) had a

clear run in deciding on the pattern of school life.

The boys rose, literally, at dawn, and had to be washed and dressed in time for prayers at seven o'clock. From nine o'clock until dinner, at one, they attended their lessons.

'*After dinner*', the headmaster recorded, '*when everyone had eaten as much as they could, they had to be ready for some violent game as soon after half-past one as possible ... a pernicious habit. At least half-an-hour should have been given to meditation. It doesn't matter what was meditated as long as we meditated and didn't ruin our young digestions*'.

Afternoon lessons started at either three o'clock or three thirty and went on until six o'clock. Thirty minutes later, tea was ready, followed – at half-past seven – by preparation.

The day ended rather abruptly with prayers at nine-thirty '*and then bed in which everybody had to be deaf and dumb by ten o'clock,*' Mr Taylor said.

For him, the day ended with one last duty. Lantern in hand, he then toured the dormitories to make certain that all was well and safe for the eight hours before another busy day began.

MOORLAND PLAYGROUND ... Today's Kelly College pupils, who now include girls as well as boys, enjoy adventure expeditions on Dartmoor in addition to the academic curriculum.

Moretonhampstead

What a drama befell a Moretonhampstead household in June 1919.

Sending a postcard to a friend in High Wycombe, a visitor wrote: *'We sat in the field behind the hedge here on Sunday to watch the faithful go to the kirk (church). I didn't feel too well yesterday as the helpings at the meals are too large. The cook ran away from here on Monday and we live on cold mutton and prunes.'*

Moreton deserves – and has – far more going for it than these few words of faith and feasting.

With its lands recorded in *Domesday*, its links reach back to the Iron Age and, through the days of William the Conqueror, to Tudor times and then onward to the present day. Its famous sons include one, George Parker Bidder, renowned as 'the calculating boy', not from any trait of manipulative character, but to an uncanny mathematical brain. He was born in 1806 and could, no sooner than the question was posed, come up with the cube foot of such figures as 304,821 and 217 or – given up to fifteen seconds – those of 67,667,921 and 875. As a young man he went to London and became a civil engineer, working with Robert Stephenson on the London to Birmingham railway project, the construction of London's Victoria Docks and the establishment of the Electric Telegraph Company.

To Moreton went the dubious honour of seeing the last English murder by a highwayman, when a Mr John May was killed by Buckingham Joe Oliver and Turpin Galley, two delightfully-named rogues. Buckingham Joe ended his days as the star of a public hanging on August 12, 1836.

Moreton was, in its day, a town of notable educational excellence

ONE VIEW OF THE ALMSHOUSES ... This is the postcard sent to a friend by the unfortunate guest who, in 1919, endured the diet of mutton and prunes ...

with, by 1844, a library and reading room; a literary society and an institute of mechanics where lectures were held weekly with the stated intention of *'advancing the learning of the lower orders of society as well as to combat heavy drinking'*. The reading room, which carried a salary of £8 per annum for its first librarian, and an £11 annual allowance for new books, was followed by a full public library given to the town by Sir Thomas Bowring.

Two fires in the nineteenth century destroyed most of Moretonhampstead's historic buildings. The devastation might not have been so severe had there not been commercial rivalry between insurance companies. The sole fire appliance was owned by the West of England Insurance Company. This meant that it remained in its station if ever fire afflicted any property either insured by a rival or, perhaps, not insured at all. In 1838, it went to the rescue of its policyholders in *The White Heart*, totally ignoring properties blazing away in Pound-street. Following this outbreak, the insurance company put up its premiums and even fewer people could then afford insurance cover. Thus the 'great fire' of 1845 completed the devastation begun seven years earlier, and robbed the town of much of its architectural heritage.

The beautiful almshouses in Cross-street, fashioned as an arcade with eleven openings, and built in 1637, miraculously survived the ravages of time and flames, as did St Andrew's church which draws the qualified praise of *'a spacious type of 15th century Moorland church which contains little of note'*. Another writer, the Rev Samuel Rowe, went as far as dismissing its *'appointments – for example, the pulpit of wood painted to imitate granite – are wretched ... the original design of the late Gothic church has been much interfered with from time to time'*.

Amongst the poignant memorials is one to Charles Tozer, who died in 1813 at the age of twenty-nine:

'A pining sickness gave the fatal blow,
the stroke was certain, but the effect was slow,
with wasting pain, Death found sore oppressed,
pitied my sighs and kindly gave me rest'.

In 1848, the Rev Samuel Rowe noted that *'the famous dancing tree of Moreton – an elm – is now sadly dwindled from its former capacious dimensions, and to all appearance will soon die'*.

AND ANOTHER ... A prettier depiction of the old buildings.

He was wrong, for it has a worthy replacement that lives.

But what is a Dancing Tree?

Throughout the nineteenth century the Dancing Tree was an old elm under which a small platform had been erected for singing and dancing (as well as for open-air drinking). It was the centre-piece for merrymaking and public jollity, particularly at carnival time. Although it finally decayed and died in the 1880s, a successor, this time a beech – took its worthy place and provides a distinguished and natural protective shade over the head of a medieval cross.

PROTECTION ... The Dancing Tree throws a leafy umbrella over the medieval cross.

Moretonhampstead   The Cross Tree

The Wrench Series No. 6537

36

The Rights, the Traditions and the Privileges of the Dartmoor Miners

A S an eighteenth-century botanist and geologist, W G Maton would have seen the best – and the worst – of the British countryside when, in 1795, he visited Devon.

Yet, travelling across Blackdown, between Mary Tavy and Lydford, he experienced something that caused him to write: '*I have never passed a more dreary tract than that over which we passed from the tin mines towards Lidford. The soil is extremely swampy and moist and covered with bog-moss through which our horses' legs penetrated knee-deep at every step. If we had not been accompanied by the captain of the mines, who seemed to be well acquainted with the country, we should have been in unceasing apprehension of sinking deeper than our heads. Though it may naturally be imagined that so wet, exposed and uncomfortable a district must be unhealthy, we were informed that the inhabitants live to an extraordinary age. They reckon themselves middle-aged only when arriving at sixty and "it is no uncommon thing" (said our guide) "to hear the death of a man of seventy years of age spoken of as if premature". The principle cause, I believe, of this longevity is the absence of temptations to intemperance*'.

Who was he trying to kid?

True, in Dartmoor villages long life was not unusual amongst those who worked the land. They drew the benefits, not of intemperance, but of fresh air, hard work and a simple but adequate diet.

Amongst miners things were very different. In addition to accident or severe injury, the humidity and damp of working long hours underground, often waist-deep in tepid water, reduced life expectancy by more than one half of those who worked above ground and a miner still alive at his 30th birthday was something to be marvelled at.

A BLEAK LANDSCAPE … But for those with the skill and courage rich pickings of minerals lay below the surface.

Sadly, Maton was not interested in the mines or the miners beyond recording that: *'From Tavistock we proceeded to Okehampton. To the right of the road, within the precincts of Dartmoor, some mines drew our attention and, farther to the right, there is a very remarkable water-fall which also led us from the high road.*

'We came first to a copper mine called Huel Friendship, situated in a valley about five miles from Tavistock. About a mile east-ward from the copper mine, we saw two tin mines, Huel Jewel and Huel Unity'.

On thing that arises from Maton's notes is that, in West Devon, the word 'mine' was described as the Welsh 'huel', the Cornish 'wheal' not being adopted for almost another fifty years – perhaps as more and more Cornishmen made their way into the mines of Dartmoor as those of the Duchy were gradually exhausted of eco-nomically-redeemable minerals.

Wheal United was the oldest and largest mine to the east of Tavistock. It was opened in 1796 and, by 1822, was being operated to a depth of 170 fathoms (340 metres). Thirteen gigantic water-wheels provided the necessary motive power and, as a standby for use in frost or drought to supplement the water-wheels, there was a powerful steam engine.

In 1844, this impressive array of power was increased by the installation of what was to be, in its day, the biggest and most powerful water-wheel in Britain, measuring 17 metres in diameter and 4 metres across.

Wheal Friendship employed over 200 men, women and young people in its ceaseless toil and was to give its investors over £286,000 in its working lifetime.

By the 1870s, the great age of Dartmoor mining was over and the population of villages like Horndon, Peter Tavy and Mary Tavy went into decline. Indeed, as various memorials and headstones show in local churchyards, the Devon miners followed their Cornish colleagues to South Africa, Australia and the Americas in search of work and a use for their skills.

At the turn of the century, Wheal Friendship was still in very limited operation. No longer was copper mined. The new task was to produce mundic, from which arsenic could be extracted for use in a range of purposes from medicines to cosmetics.

For amateur criminologists who regard arsenic as a popular way of committing murder, it might come hard to learn that the substance actually had health-giving as well as life-taking characteristics, and could be used in tonics prescribed for nerve disorders, as a sheep dip, and for the special soap used by taxidermists when treating the dead bodies of animals prior to stuffing them.

An official notice exhibited in places where arsenic was mined, processed or used warned: *'Persons who work in the preparation of arsenic are liable to poisoning. Powerful emetics and a stomach pump must be instantly available. Causes of persons being wilfully poisoned by doses of arsenic have been fairly frequent. However, it is readily detected in the body after death'.*

Traditionally, like their cousins in Cornwall, the Dartmoor miners had their own parliament after the two groups separated prior to the days of Edward I, in the thirteenth century.

The Devonshire 'members of parliament' were called 'jurats', whereas the Cornish equivalent were 'stannators'.

ANCIENT PARLIAMENT ... Crockern Tor.

Maton tried to compare the two systems of Devon and Cornwall, and concluded: *'The Devon laws, with regard to mining, seem to have never been so well defined, or so equitable, as those which respect the Cornishmen, but – both being included in the Duchy of Cornwall – are under the same constitution. One general warden called the Lord Warden of the Stannaries, either by himself or his deputy, has the supreme decision in matters of both law and equity, relative to the tin mines of the duchy. A court is generally holden once a month by the sub-warden, who receives appeals from inferior courts, wherein officers preside, but a jury is impanelled on all occasions.*

'No laws are valid unless passed in a stannary parliament to which every stannary town sends six representatives. Every Act must be signed by these representatives, the Lord Warden, or his deputy, and lastly by the Duke himself (in his privy council) or the sovereign, and has then the

authority with regard to tin affairs of an Act of the supreme legislature of England'.

The Devonshire jurats, Maton said: *'meet on Dartmore mountain at a place called Crockern Tor, in the parish of Wydecomb, where there is a stone table and single stones round for the members to sit on, from which place they adjourn to do business'.*

Indeed, Crockern Tor could be so inhospitable in the cold and wet of a Dartmoor day, that the jurats – twenty-four from Tavistock, Ashburton, Plympton and Chagford would usually only stay at their stone table for as long as it took formally to open the session before beating a hasty retreat to the more hospitable and comfortable surroundings of Tavistock.

But why was it necessary to have a special parliament for the miners?

In those far-off days, the skills of mining were already rare and keenly sought-after. In order to secure the best-possible manpower, employers were only too happy to grant various privileges.

Tinners were allowed to 'bound' an area, by marking out a parcel to be worked for minerals either by small holes and heaps of turf, or by erecting poles topped with a furze bush. They were allowed unimpeded rights to dig wherever tin might be found; to bring water to the site; exemption from tithes and dues; and immunity from military service.

It was as these traditional rights came under pressure that they required their own forum to safeguard their hard-earned privileges against those who clearly had a vested interest in reducing or violating them.

One of the problems was that the landowners tried to sidestep the stannary rules by claiming that as they owned mineral areas, the laws should not apply to them!

The parliament nipped this one in the bud by ruling that anyone owning mineral workings or other related estate, with an income of more than £10 a year, should not be allowed to work tin – thus eliminating the 'capitalists'. However, as the effective working of the stannary parliaments had to depend on the influence and goodwill of the wealthy landowners, the '£10 rule' was abandoned.

The first recorded session at Crockern Tor was on September 14 1494. As documents were never kept, there is no record of how

DARTMOOR CHARACTER ... The sturdy determination of working folk is clearly stamped on the faces of this couple, Mr and Mrs Cleave and their little daughter as they pose, at Merripit, for Robert Burnard, the gifted Devon photographer.

proceedings progressed or, indeed, of what proposals were rejected or ignored. The only hint lies in the various beliefs and traditions that have survived the years.

What was interesting, however, was the way in which the jurats and stannators realised the delicacy of their position. On the one hand it was one of virtually absolute power. On the other, it was vulnerable to exploitation by themselves and could always be rescinded if they went over the top.

Therefore, whilst pursuing their rights and freedoms without respite, they were ruthless in self-discipline in such measures as tax-avoidance, criminal offences and the adulteration of tin by the addition of impurities to increase the weight but reduce the quality.

It was the key issue of quality that led to the creation of the so-called 'Stannary towns' where tin was brought to be weighed, tested for purity and stamped. Clearly there was a temptation to tamper with the tin since most working tinners were farm-labourers who, with a pick and shovel, a bucket and a promising watercourse, 'streamed' for tin. The individual yield would be low and, at best, provide only a small secondary income.

The tin could only be stamped twice a year and as it was illegal to sell it before it had been stamped, the labourers were at the mercy of tin dealers who would – illegally – buy small quantities of unstamped tin at knock-down prices from those who were too poor, or too impatient, to await the next stamping-day.

As Dr W G Hoskins points out, in *Devon: 'It was still mainly a small man's trade. The big capitalist has appeared on the scene ... but there is still ample room for small working partnerships, and even for the lone adventurer toiling with pick and shovel at his own claim: the immemorial bowed figure of solitary man, working in the vast silence of the Moor as his ancestors had done in the Cornish wastes three thousand years before'.*

The Devon tinners' parliament sat for the last recorded time, at Crockern Tor, in 1749. Within a comparatively few years all traces of the stone table and the stone seats had gone. The suspicion is that they were carted off by a Mr Gullett, the owner of Prince Hall, and were recycled in the interests of agriculture and the comfort of cattle needing a good scratch.

But the image of the tinner's parliament is kept alive by this description – dating back to its final days – : *'On this tor was a warden's or president's chair, seats for the jurats, a high corner stone for the crier of the court, and a table – all roughly hewn out of the rough moorstone of the tor, together with a cavern which, for the convenience of our modern courts, was used in these latter ages, as a repository for wine'.*

ENGINE HOUSE … Wheal Betsy at Mary Tavy, recently restored by conservation bodies under the auspices of Dartmoor National Park.

Lydford Prison –
'Contagious and Detestable'

IT WAS a clash with the tinners' parliament that led to Richard Strode, MP for Plympton, into a prison more feared than Tyburn, Newgate or even the Tower of London.

It led, too, to British members of parliament being granted the privilege of being allowed to speak in the course of parliamentary debate, without fear of sanction, fine, imprisonment or incurring any external penalty.

The tinners' parliament, by attempting to curb freedom of speech, not only guaranteed it, but also drew attention to Britain's blackest prison – Lydford.

Richard Strode infringed the presumed rights and dignities of the parliament at Crockern Tor when, in a speech at Westminster, he dared to suggest that tinners were responsible for the silting-up of neighbouring harbours.

Amongst the rights granted to tinners were those of access to waterways, watercourses and harbours. However, tin-production led to the silting-up of some ports and, representing the interests of shippers, seamen and other users of maritime transport, Richard Strode introduced a Bill in 1512. Arguing for its acceptance, he violated stannary statute and was accused of obstructing the rights of tinners.

He was summoned to Crockern Tor but, adding insult to injury, he declined to appear. In a fine old state of fury at what it regarded as contempt as well as damage to its authority, the court fined him the statutory maximum of £40 *'to be inflicted upon any who do obstruct tinners in their rights'*.

Not appreciating the powers of the stannary parliament as being greater than those of Westminster, Strode ignored the conviction

CENTRES OF POWER ... Lydford Church and the castle in 1820.

and the fine and then, rashly, returned to Plympton.

As he crossed Dartmoor he was arrested and thrown into the stannary prison at Lydford.

Lydford castle, which dates from the thirteenth century, had been designated the official stannary prison soon after Edward I had granted Dartmoor's tinners their own rights and powers.

The dungeon was a dark pit some five metres by five metres. It was windowless. There was only one way in – down a ladder. As the governor was only required to produce prisoners at the Assizes at Exeter once every ten years, the majority of inmates were dead long before they were tried or their sentences reviewed.

There were only three ways out – death, luck or money.

Richard Strode chose the latter and, in return for £100 deposited with the deputy-warden of the Stannaries, Thomas Denys, he was released and able to return to Westminster where he described his incarnation in: *'one of the most anncious, contagious and destestable places wythen this realme.'*

He wasted no time in introducing a Bill granting all parliamentarians privilege to make statements – however disparaging, hurtful, malicious or inaccurate – in the House without external answerability, thus establishing that Westminster authority was greater than that of outside bodies.

Lydford castle dates back some nine hundred years and was one of the four castles in Devon dating back to Norman times. Indeed, alongside Exeter, Barnstaple and Totnes, Lydford shares the honour of being one of Devon's four oldest boroughs – although its prosperity and importance were shortlived with the growth of Okehampton, Tavistock and Launceston.

During his visit, in 1795, W G Maton found that Lydford had become so poor that it had been excused, on grounds of poverty, from sending representatives to parliament: *'a plea which the present appearance of it seems to have fairly justified them in making for it has dwindled into a small shabby village'*.

The castle had become: *'a square building of an unmeaning appearance, being without strength or ornament'*.

How the mighty had fallen!

A century earlier, executions had been commonplace in this grim jail, the victims being hung in chains and, to make the lesson of

LYDFORD CASTLE … 'A contagious and detestable place.'

WATERFALL … The famous Whitelady fall at Lydford Gorge.

judicial murder last as long as possible, the corpses were dipped in tar to delay decomposition for as long as possible ... earning a ghastly reputation enshrined in the words of the poet, William Browne, in 1644:

'I oft have heard of Lydford law –
how in the morning they hang and draw
– and sit in judgment after.
At first I wondered at it much;
but, since, I've found the matter such
that it deserves no laughter'.

In 1650, an official survey of prisons classified Lydford as 'dilapidated' but – up to the early 1800s – according to William Crossing, it was in 'tolerable repair'.

If the evil prison and castle dominate the historic reality of Lydford, then its other great feature, its gorge, captures the timeless beauty of nature.

According to one local writer two centuries ago: *'It maketh such a hideous noise that, being only heard and not seen, it causeth a kind of fear, seeming to them that look down to it a great abyss; and may be numbered among the wonders of this kingdom'.*

Doctor Richard Pockocke saw it this way, in 1750: *'The rock, being uneven on each side, and the river working down under the bridge in beautiful cascades. About a mile higher up, the rocks are so close that the river seems to fall down out of a hole in the rock'.*

And the words of the Rev S Shaw, writing in 1788: *'Winding down the rock, on a small path about half way, you are presented by the finest milky streams imaginable, neither too perpendicular to be one confused heap, nor too much divided to be ungraceful; but one continued silvery chain of 200 feet; towards the bottom the rock projects so favourable as to fill the air with aqueous particles, and imitate the effect of a real fountain, softly falling in a silver shower. Descending beneath, you look up on the whole with a similar enchantment. This surprising waterfall pleased me altogether more than any in the North of England or Scotland, and being a greater rarity in these parts, it is more valuable and striking'.*

Perhaps less valuable than the gorge – but every bit as striking – was the Gubbins family which reputedly lurked in its darkest recesses some four hundred years ago. Like the Doones of Exmoor, they robbed, rampaged, raped and ravaged.

They were easily recognised by their red beards. They spoke a strange gibberish dialect of their own; could outrun a horse; and escaped every attempt to hunt them down. When, eventually, they became extinct, it was said to be due to inbreeding and excessive alcoholic abuse rather than judicial vengeance.

Perhaps though they merely blended into respectable anonymity rather than disappearing from the face of legendary humanity. A rector of Lydford, the Rev Morris Fuller, seemed to detect some sign of social integration when, in the 1640s, he noted: *'I am informed that they begin to be civilised, and tender their children to baptism; and return to be men, yea Christians again'.*

RUGGED COUNTRY ... The moorland which once harboured gangs of brigands.

50

RIVER CROSSING … A slender bridge spans part of Lydford Gorge.

The Railways Came ... and the Trains Went

RAILWAYS across Dartmoor arrived in a blaze of controversy in the middle of the nineteenth century and were laid to rest in overrated awe and nostalgia about one hundred years later, their passing marked with the same fervent arguments for retention as marked the campaign against them in the first place.

Railways, it seemed, marked a colourful interlude – almost an outbreak of eccentricity in the Moor's pattern of transport.

In the 1850s, the arguments in favour of railways were that they were needed to guarantee transport links between Moor and the fringe towns; that they would be cheap and therefore well used; that they would be reliable irrespective of weather conditions; and that they would pave the way for the development of tourism. The counter-argument was that they would be smelly and noisy; unreliable; likely to frighten livestock and – above all – would introduce a wholly alien culture to the Moor.

In the 1960s, they had outlived their popularity; they went – in the main – to the wrong places for the wrong reasons; had become increasingly expensive to run and maintain; and the mobility of tourism was increasingly dictated by the availability of rubber tyres rather than rails and iron wheels to travel between mandatory fixed centres.

And as to the all-weather reliability, well, the last train on the Plymouth to Tavistock line, in 1962, was the penultimate final train rather than the last train itself. Fierce snowfalls and drifting – not to mention the inevitable freezing of points – meant that the penultimate scheduled train was so delayed that it became the last one to run from Plymouth to Tavistock. It was a nightmare journey for railway buffs, little realising that their arrival in Tavistock

LAST PUFF ... The last steam train from Okehampton to Bude on a line which finally closed in 1967.

would be delayed by many cold and uncomfortable hours, consuming the hot drinks, sandwiches and contents of pocket flasks that should have been saved as a barrier against the unsuspected greater physical challenge and tests of endurance lurking ahead.

At Tavistock, many hours later, the survivors of the epic journey were greeted by enthusiastic Civil Defence workers who were able to prove the maxim of many years theoretical instruction, namely that vast quantities of soup could be brewed in galvanised dustbins.

Each 'last run' was packed with enthusiasts. With pocket watches, notebooks and timetables at the ready, they would calculate the actual and elapsed time of the journey and compare it with columns of 'best ever' times and records. With tape recorders at the ready, they would capture the sound of the train passing over famous sets of points, clattering through deserted stations, drumming over bridges, or the staccato machine-gun-like echoes as the train passed a line of stationary trucks at a junction or in a siding. Wreaths would be hung on the front of the engine and streamers would fly from windows.

Some passengers would even persuade the ever-obliging driver to stop fifty yards or so from a station, lay detonators on the tracks and then approach the platform puffing, whistling and setting-off explosions like a twenty-one gun salute ... all to be faithfully committed to posterity on miles of magnetic sound-recorded tape. At some stations there would be the added bonus of the presence of the council, the civic head and the local band to give an even greater feeling of a moment of ultimate pomp and circumstance.

The last train ran from Okehampton to Bude on May 1961, the complete line having been finally opened in 1898 after a false start which had restricted the line to the Meldon Junction to Holsworthy section since 1879. Its traffic was a mix of people and goods, much of it over the shorter intermediate sectors of the route. It carried coal and explosives from Bude to the quarries of the heartlands, as well as ballast and other forms of stone to the quays of the Cornish port. It carried, too, its loads of livestock and produce.

The last steam train, in 1961, carried the traditional 'mixed' coaches with goods capacity at one end, two first class compartments (one smoking and one non-smoking) and six third class compartments to each coach.

After the withdrawal of the steam service, the branch line continued with diesel locomotives until 1967.

Dartmoor's first railway was opened by the Moretonhampstead and South Devon Railway Company in 1866. The company was not altogether popular with the local farmers as, when a farmworker was considered well paid at 45 pence per week, the railway paid its labourers 65 pence plus overtime. Even worse, it provided an affordable way for rural dwellers to take jobs in town as well as giving their wives access to lower prices in shops in the larger towns

Over the Moors from Widecombe to Haytor. 79796A. FRITH'S

CROSSROADS ... This shepherd takes his flock on its way by the traditional moorland road – but his wife could journey by train to town for her shopping.

and freedom from generally higher prices in village shops and markets.

The South Devon Railway Company was not particularly innovative and it only really became successful when, soon after 1871, it was amalgamated with the Great Western Railway, thus opening the door to interlinking with other services, a wider selection of locomotives and rolling-stock and a marketing strategy that included running connecting buses from stations to villages.

This was indeed a contrast with the original laid-back friendly company that operated from an austere and rather dowdy wooden-shed station and rarely expected its passengers to pay to travel.

Dartmoor was also well-served by other companies, providing stations or halts at Lydford, Brentor, Tavistock, Yelverton, Mary Tavy, Ingra Tor, King Tor and Princetown, to name but a famous few.

The Princetown-Yelverton line, opened in 1883, travelled for part of its route over the original iron road built by Sir Thomas Tyrwhitt. Originally intended to carry granite and coal, the more

GETTING THROUGH … This engine has met a traditional Dartmoor weather hazard – its bowler hatted-passengers may have a long wait.

basic commodities were increasingly replaced by a human cargo as the people of Plymouth began to realise the recreational potential of Dartmoor. King Tor Halt, opened in 1928, was designed as a personal facility for men and their families associated with the adjacent quarry. Ingra Tor Halt, opened in 1936, enjoyed a certain spine-chilling notoriety in that the numerous official notices exhibited on its platform included one warning passengers of snakes.

The branch finally closed in 1956, the car having replaced the train as a more convenient means of travel. The old branch line, like so many of its fellows, passed with dignity and sad celebration, it needing two garlanded engines to haul six crammed coaches on the last run on March 5, 1956. As if confirming that there would never be a reconsideration or a reprieve, British Rail dismantled the track in the following year.

Amongst the many who were to mourn the passing of steam trains would be Devon's voluntary firemen. They could literally set their watches by the time the first message reached them that a train, stoking up the boiler to puff its way up an incline, was spewing sparks on to tinder-dry stubble or bracken and had started an impressive but fast-running fire.

For those receiving a turn-out fee, the spark-spreading locomotive was indeed an ally during the long weeks of a parched summer, the proceeds certainly being recycled in village shop or pub.

Gorse fires, too, were to be expected during the month of March. Okehampton volunteer fire brigade were in action at Ball Hill in 1926 after driving their solid-tyred machine to an outbreak. Although well-equipped by the standards of the day, many a modern window cleaner nowadays carries a more impressive array of ladders and hoses ... but without the impressive and highly-polished brass bell that demanded absolute priority over all other road users.

The fire engine was owned by the council, at Okehampton, and was a replacement for the former horse-drawn tender that had just come to a spectacular and untimely end.

Quartered in the Market Hall, the horse-drawn vehicle was destroyed when a fire that broke out in the adjacent fried fish shop spread out of control and, to the embarrassment of the firemen, also consumed cherished equipment. The horses were not at risk as they were borrowed on a 'per occasion' basis from a neighbouring squire and had to be collected, taken to the fire station and harnessed-up before the firemen could respond to the emergency call.

Ball Hill was regularly the scene of fires, not all of them caused by accident. To small boys, totally unaware of the damage they might cause, it was often very tempting – almost traditional – to get a fire going just to have the thrill of seeing the fire brigade at work.

Dartmoor – or to be more accurate, Meldon – boasts one proud railway record. It not only has one of the only two trussed-girder viaducts in the whole of Britain, but also marks the highest point on the entire Southern Region of British Railways. Crossing the valley of the West Okement, the viaduct is technically-described as: *'built on a curve of thirty chains, with girder spans supported by metal lattice piers, the tallest being one-hundred-and-twenty feet (thirty-nine metres). Its appearance is slight, and aesthetically, something looking readier to withstand the elements, preferably built of local materials, would be more in harmony with the Moor'.*

Allowing for the height of the foundations above sea level, the actual overall elevation of the viaduct is nine-hundred-and-eighty feet (three hundred-and-thirty metres).

The train pictured crossing the viaduct in the 1920s, has a general 'mix' of passenger and freight cars, together with cattle wagons at the back.

The ruins to the left of the foot of the viaduct are connected with the former lime-workings, the ruins of the lime-kiln appearing prominently.

Chagford

Few towns anywhere in Britain – and certainly on Dartmoor – give greater proof to the saying the 'beauty is in the eye of the beholder' than Chagford. Described by one writer as 'dull and uninteresting' it is 'immaculate, sturdy and calm' to another, wresting forth the description 'neat, beautiful and picturesque' from a third.

As always, the truth most probably lies somewhere in between the excesses of written description.

Certainly it's an old township and takes its name from 'chag', the old dialect word for broom or gorse, and ford. The original ford lies under the bridge that now crosses the Teign – and is the successor of bridges dating back at least eight hundred years. Leland, antiquary to King Henry VIII, had the task of searching for records of antiquity in cathedrals, colleges, abbeys and priories in England and, between 1534 and 1540, he responded by providing the king with 'a whole world of things very memorable'.

Amongst these facts and figures was a reference to the existing bridge.

Chagford itself stands in a proud position on a hill well above the breathtakingly beautiful River Teign. Its history is long and proud. When man first came to Dartmoor, he paused to build hut circles, kists and stone rows nearby. When he worked tin, he came to Chagford with the precious ore for valuation and verification. He tended his sheep nearby, and brought the wool to Chagford. If he bought, or sold, then Chagford was the place.

By the 1300s it was a centre of commerce and influence.

By the 1400s it could boast a proud church – St Michael's. It would carry proud monuments to Sir John Whiddon and to John Prouz.

Sir John, who died in 1575, was a justice of the Queen's Bench. He was the owner of the manor of Chagford and Whiddon Park, a couple of miles from the town itself. The park is described as being *'romantically beautiful, a place of rocks, ravens and wild deer. The house is substantially Elizabethan, and attractive'*.

In the town itself, the striking *Three Crowns Inn* was built in the early 1500s as the town centre developed in an era of great and growing local prosperity.

It was at *The Three Crowns*, in February 1643, that Sidney Godolphin is reputed to have been killed. Godolphin, a member of a great Cornish family, was an officer in King Charles' army. Chagford was one of the many Dartmoor towns that supported Cromwell's troops.

Under Sir John Berkeley, a group of royalists attacked their adversaries taking refuge in Chagford. In a brief battle, the royalists were victorious. However, their military victory was overshadowed by the loss of Godolphin.

Sir Bevill Grenville, one of Charles' more brilliant commanders, realised that the royalist army in Cornwall was in danger of being denied vital supplies by the parliamentary blockade of Devon. At Braddock Down, Grenville's army broke through and set out to pursue the retreating Roundheads. Grenville later wrote: *'a small force set off in pursuit through Okehampton towards Totnes, but when they entered Chagford in the early morning, they found a parliamentary force there and fierce fighting ensured. Worst of all, a chance shot from an unseen foe hit Sidney Godolphin in the thigh, and with a cry of "Oh God, I am hurt", he fell dead from his horse'.*

Writing some seven months after the event, Clarendon added a little more to Grenville's terse report. *'We lost Sidney Godolphin, a young gentleman of incomparable parts. He received a mortal shot by a musket a little above the knee, of which he died on the instant, leaving the misfortune of his death upon a place which could never otherwise have had a mention in the world'.*

Chagford, Clarendon suggested, would have remained an anonymous place were it not for Godolphin's death.

But, had it not been for Chagford, would anyone have remembered Sydney Godolphin?

CHAGFORD.

YEARS AGO ... A peaceful view of Chagford.

61

Walla Brook Bridge. Chagford

TWO BRIDGES ... Walla Brook Bridge, and below, Chagford Bridge, seen on postcards dated early this century.

Chagford Bridge

It seems that he was destined for great things and that his death gave a massive boost to Roundhead morale equally balanced by the blow caused to the high spirits of the conquering Cavaliers. Again, to quote Grenville: *'our men were forced to retire again after they were in: and one loss that we have sustained that is invaluable, to wit, Sidney Godolphin is slain in the attempt, who was as gallant a gentleman as the world had'*.

A few days later there was a break in the bitter civil war. In what was to become a most uneasy and suspicious truce, an agreement was signed at Tavistock establishing a three-week peace whereby 'no actual warfare shall occur in Devon and Cornwall'.

Grenville and the royalists used the respite to raise funds and redeploy their men in strategic positions. Meanwhile, Sir George Chudleigh, parliamentary commander in Devon, admitted that his side were doing much the same thing, adding *'we are now again at our wonted enmity, each county performing and drawing forces to the borders for a new invasion'*.

The civil war ended and Chagford returned to peaceful days. The local markets flourished, selling food, clothing and pots and pans. Four major cattle fairs became fixtures in the calendar.

As late as the mid-1800s, canny housewives found they could get real bargains if they delayed their actual spending until the last minutes of market day when traders, faced with either selling cheaply or else risking produce going off, would sell at knockdown price.

But despite its prosperity and its promise, Chagford's development peaked in about 1831 and its great rival, Moretonhampstead – arguably – increased its successful challenge.

Moretonhampstead acquired the railway and Chagford had to make do with a connecting bus service. As trade contracted, so the new Dartmoor industry of tourism reached out its tentacles and the historic town became a mecca for those seeking exercise, visual splendour and the bracing moorland air.

Recalling the findings of the clergyman, the Rev Samuel Rowe, who noted that in Chagford during a 'perambulation' in 1848, *'a post-chaise at the door of* The Three Crowns *is sufficiently of wonder to attract a group of rustic onlookers'*, William Crossing found half-a-century later that *'during the summer season Chagford is full of visitors, and can boast of good hotels and boarding houses. The air of picturesque informality in its appearance of which Mr Rowe speaks, has certainly not altogether vanished, but it is not quite so striking as in his time, or within our own recollection. And the quaint costume of the ancient dames, to which he also alludes, are no longer to be seen in the street, or at church, modern fashions of dress having taken their place ... The town has shown itself ambitious, too, for a few years since it witnessed the installation of electric light. Thus Chagford in one respect has outstripped the capital of the Moor, for Princetown has still to be content with gas'.*

MOORLAND CROSS ... Week Down. ▶

FROZEN IN SUMMERTIME ... A photograph taken in 1890 of a ▶
rose-covered cottage in Throwleigh. Two patient horses wait outside, pet-ted by two ladies wearing the bustles of the time.

ROSE COTTAGE ... A pony and trap wait outside this pretty cottage, depict-ed on an old postcard.

Chagford, Rose Cottage.

CHAGFORD .1157   WEEK DOWN CROSS

How St Joan Became the Live-In Saint of Tavistock's Goosie Fair

IT MAY be approaching its five hundredth anniversary and it may not show the same vitality that once was its hallmark.

But references to the terminal decline, or predictions of its demise, are both premature and exaggerated for Tavistock Goosie Fair – or 'Tavystock Goozey Vair' as C John Trythall's famous song would have it – shows no signs of joining Britain's growing list of former national fetes, fairs and festivals.

Some four hundred and fifty years ago, what was to become the Tavistock goose fair was firmly set in the annual calendar as one of the privileges granted by Tavistock Abbey's authorities to the rural church of St Michael's, Brentor.

St Michael's Day – Michaelmas – fell on September 29 and Brentor enjoyed three days of celebration.

However, when the Earl of Bedford reorganised local diary dates after the dissolution of the monasteries in the mid-1500s, he decided that Brentor's festivities should be rescheduled to join Tavistock's four great fairs. So as not to be accused of being purely interested in the tolls and levies collected from traders and sellers, the Earl softened the blow by saying that he would pocket the proceeds from two of them, but that the cash from the other three would go into the funds of the recently-restored grammar school.

There was, though, still the delicate matter of squeezing the Michaelmas event into a pretty packed couple of months. In September there was already one great event – St John's Fair – which specialised in the sale of sheep and cattle together with corn and other cereal crops.

In a spot of marketing wizardry well ahead of his day, the Earl decided that the new event would be called 'St Joan's Fair'. As he saw it, nobody could confuse St John with St Joan and, with an eye to undreamed-of feminism still some four hundred years over the horizon, he unashamedly introduced a policy of attracting the wives, mothers, sisters and daughters to what would be a relaxed occasion as much of interest to the women as to their menfolk and gave the whole event an air of celebration for the end of harvest.

Since, however, Michaelmas Day was one on which rent had to be paid, farmers and smallholders were grateful for a special market at which they could sell any surplus geese to raise the ready-money for their rent.

It was, in fact, both painless and simple.

That was until a 'new' calendar was introduced in 1752. It had the rather dramatic effect of shortening the year by eleven days. Consequently, September 29 became October 10 and, thus Tavistock claimed that date – irrespective of the day of the week on which it fell – as the day of Goose Fair. In a further rationalisation, it was decided in 1822 firmly to schedule the event for the second Wednesday of October, irrespective of the actual date.

In 1780, in his October visit to the town, the Rev S. Shaw found that: *this being market day, we met numbers of people flocking hither with grain, a few sheep and an abundance of Michaelmas geese*.

The unofficial version of the naming of the event is colourful, but shared with Nottingham, which boasts its goose fair one week earlier.

According to this yarn, a farmer from the heart of Dartmoor brought up his three sons totally isolated from the sight or influence of women after their mother died while they were still infants.

He did such a good job that when, eventually, the three strapping and lusty young men were introduced to the maidens of Tavistock, he was at a loss to explain what ladies were when the boys spotted some and asked what they were, what was their use, and why did they seem to be different from men?

The proud dad asked his sons what they would like as a souvenir of their visit to Tavistock.

'What are those?' they asked, pointing to some pouting and pulchritudinous persons.

'They', replied the father, 'are geese'.

"Tavvystock Goozey Vair"

Words and Music:

C. John Trythall

No. I in F

No. 2 in G.

J. H. LARWAY,

Proprietors : EDWIN ASHDOWN, LTD.,

19, HANOVER SQUARE, LONDON, W.1

MADE AND PRINTED IN ENGLAND.

TAVVYSTOCK GOOZEY VAIR.

Words and Music by

C. JOHN TRYTHALL.

VOICE.

PIANO.

just a month cum Vri - day nex' Bill Champ - er - nown an' me____ Us

druv' a crost ole Dar - ty - moor th' Goo - zey Vair to zee.____ Us

L.1548ª

made our-sels quite 'vit-ty'___ Us__ shav'd and grais'd our 'air___ An'

off us goes in our Zun-day cloes be-'ind__Bill's ole gray mare.___ Us

smell'd the sage an' on-ions_ arl th' way fr'm Whit-church Down,___ An'

didn' us av a blaw-out when us put up in th' town,___ An'

L. 15484

theer us met Ned 'An-na-furd, Jan Steer an' Nick-y Square,— Ut

sim to we arl Deb'm mus' be to Tav-vy-stock Goo-zey Vair.— An' uts

Aw thun, whur be'e gwaine,— an' wot be'e do-in' of there?— 'Aive

down yer prong, an' stap down long, tes Tav-vy-stock Goo-zey Vair.—

went an' zeed th' 'oss - es, an' th' yaf - fers, an' th' yaws,____ Us
rain - in' straims an' dark as pitch when us start - ed 'ome that night____ An'

went 'pun arl th' round - a - bouts an' in - ter arl th' shaws____ An'
when us got pas' Mer - ri - val Birdge' th' mare er tuk a vright____ Says

then ut start - ed rain - in'____ 'an____ blaw - in' too, Es Fai,____ So
I to Bill, "Be care - ful____ er you'll av us in th' drains"____ Says

L. 15484

72

the roundabouts

off us goes back to th' 'Rose' an' 'aves a dish o' tay___ An'
Bill ter me, "Be - gad," says 'e, "Why, abm' yew got th' reins?" Just

then us 'ad a zing - zong an' th' folks kep' drap - pin' in.___ An'
then th' mare run slap a - gin__ a whack - in' gurt big stoan___ 'Er

them wot knaw'd us arl cum roun' an' 'ad a drap o' gin___ Till
kicked th' trap to flib - bits an__ 'er trot - ted off a - lone___ When

wot with one an' t'oth - er___ us .. did - n' sim to care___ So us
us cum to us reck - in'd___ twarnt no gude set - tin' there___ So us

L.15488

73

Tes Tavvystock Goozey Vair

7

L.15488   LOWE & BRYDONE PRINTERS LTD, LONDON, N.W. 10

74

'Then can we have some geese please?', the boys asked.

The fair gradually dwindled from the three days of the 1500s to the early 1800s to become a two-day event, the first day being traditionally 'town day' and the second day attended by visitors. Sadly, too, the moral tone began to fall as it attracted cheats, pickpockets, card-sharpers and harlots to the rich pickings so conveniently brought together for their ingenuity to exploit.

In 1869, one traditionalist warned, in a letter to a local newspaper: *'Before many years are passed, the fair will have vanished altogether'*. Five years later another prophet of doom opined that it was *'approaching extinction'*.

Another detractor used Victorian pomposity and eloquence to note: *'It stands on tottering legs which are yearly growing weaker'*.

Certainly while everyone did their best to reverse the decline, their efforts were often counter-productive. Publicans brought in entertainers, but had to remove doors and window frames to make it easier to eject the alcoholically legless. Those who failed the 'test your strength' machines could still show off their presumed prowess by indulging in street-corner fisticuffs with drunks. And it was perhaps merciful to the easily-scandalised that the guttering flares and torches of the official attractions did not penetrate the darkness too deeply at the back of the stalls and stands!

Indeed, one indignant citizen was so outraged in 1900 that he wrote to Tavistock town council: *'I take the liberty of asking your honourable council if your influence can be exerted towards the suppression of some of the many evils connected with the present keeping of Goose Fair in Tavistock. To me, as a recent resident, it seems like the retention of old barbarous customs that there should be such scenes on this day and that the vilest women from Plymouth and Devonport should be allowed to act as they do. I am informed that the worst cases of bastardy are attributed to this annual debauchery'*.

His utterances had an unintended result. On the maxim that there is no such thing as bad publicity, the new few years saw an increase in attendance by sailors from Plymouth, marines from Stonehouse, whores from St Budeaux all joining together in a colourful congregation including teetotallers from Gunnislake, farmers from Bridestowe and Jack-the-Lads from Lifton and Lewdown.

It was said that, in 1915, soldiers camped nearby who had been battle-trained for France were so disgusted and ashamed of the drunkeness they had seen *'in inns that have become the setting for scenes of degradation and depravity'* that, sickened and embarrassed, they made their way early back to their bivouacs.

Control was clearly needed and, soon after the Great War, the council took the fair by the scruff of its very tarnished neck and banned sideshows exploiting freaks and deformities; acts subjecting animals to indignity; and introduced a total prohibition of any entertainment, show or exhibition involving, or implying 'females scantily attired and partaking in performances of an immodest nature'.

But if all these wild scenes of immodest, lewd and lascivious behaviour were taking place, then where were the police?

Perhaps the answer was given to the local magistrates in 1873 when, at the trial of a local publican convicted of allowing his premises to be used for the purposes of prostitution, no fewer than three policemen were called to give evidence.

But did the alleged degradation, exploitation and depravity ever go far beyond the titillating publicity of the imaginative showmen? And was it not the case that only a fool would take it on trust that the attraction would really justify its lurid description?

Were the cavorting 'giant' children really small adults? Were the 'dwarfs' not, perhaps, children? Did the bears and monkeys really dance? And how many of the misty 'memories of the old days' owed their foundation to the ministrations of the innkeepers rather than the artistry of the acts?

And wasn't it all really rather innocent, with stalls offering nothing more debauched than gingerbreads, sweets, pies and toys? And weren't the temporary theatres brought alive by tragical men and tinselled ladies sad rather than salacious?

Indeed, just which year is described in these words, 1845, 1945 or 1994? – : *'In one corner the vendor dispenses his wares, reducing the high price on one article shilling by shilling till at last, clapping something additional upon it, he offers the two for a shilling and clenches the temptation with the generous offer that if anyone can buy them cheaper in the shops he will actually give him the whole for nothing; whilst in another quarter the air is pierced with the shrill music of hurdy-gurdies, tambourines and*

"the human voice divine" of sun-browned foreign girls ...'.
Another fair? Another town? Another year?

Perhaps the only glaring difference lies in the cost of providing the escapism and paraphernalia of the fair. In 1845, counting plywood stalls, oiled tarpaulins, guttering flares and open fires for hot snacks, the 'value' of Tavistock Goosie Fair would have come to a total investment of less than £3000. Yet, with health, hygiene, safety, taste and novelty considerations becoming critical in a demanding, sophisticated and electronic modern world, just one of the 'rides' featured in 1993 represented an outlay of some £250,000.

Another thing that hasn't changed through the years is the unwritten – but wholly-observed – custom that, like Cinderella's night at the ball, everything came to an end at midnight.

As the church clock struck, Tavistock threw off its mantle of uninhibited enjoyment, gathered its cloak of respectability and responsibility closely about it ... and acknowledged the crispness of an autumn night and the storing of another treasury of happy memories.

ROAD TO THE FAIR ... To fun and frolics – or debauchery and depravity?

Ashburton

To say of any town that it is a good place for retirement might be seen as a double edged compliment. Yet in the case of Ashburton it is a fitting tribute in more ways than one.

As a town its importance and vigour have passed into discreet and delicate retirement; its way of life is less hectic than that of many of its neighbours; and for taking life gently and for using each day for gentle exploration and exercise, it provides opportunities that cannot be seriously challenged by any of its Dartmoor rivals.

Taking its name from the stream on which it was founded – the Ashburn (now more commonly known as the Yeo) – Ashburton owed its founding and much of its growth to the bishops of Exeter from the days of the Normans until those of James I. Indeed its importance in both agriculture and the working of minerals had been recognised by designating it a borough in the early 1200s.

As the tin trade grew, so did Ashburton's prosperity and importance. Alongside Chagford, Plympton and Tavistock, it became a stannary town. Like its fellows on the other three corners of Dartmoor, it became an official collection point for the sampling, weighing and official stamping of tin before it could be sold.

Not wishing to put all its economic eggs in one basket, Ashburton also encouraged the development of the cloth trade, in the sixteenth and seventeenth centuries. During these years, the river Ashburn was used to wash raw wool as well as to power a number of 'fulling' mills where cloth was cleaned and thickened. Cattle and corn were added to its market activities and, by the mid-1500s it was accorded the right to hold two important annual fairs.

QUIET TOWN ... Ashburton in a peaceful era.

The opening of the main road from Plymouth to Exeter saw Ashburton firmly established, in the late seventeenth century, as the geographical halfway house between the two centres of importance. Sadly, it did not seem to develop its full potential and was rather dismissively recorded by Celia Fiennes, in 1698, as *'this Ashburton is a poor little town – bad was the best inn'*.

Perhaps Celia was prejudiced. How could she have failed to comment on the attractive old houses in the town, many of them slatehung in accordance with the local tradition?

How, too, could she have overlooked the even-then historic St Andrews church, dating back to the fifteenth century and accepted as one of the most magnificent in that part of Devon? Indeed, some of the church that existed in the days of Celia Fiennes most probably originated in the 1300s if not a decade or two earlier.

It was carefully restored during the eighteenth century but, alas, much of the original was lost in the course of restoration. Some of the beautiful screens were sold for firewood, with other unique artefacts being classified as useless and sold to neighbouring churches at a knock-down price. Amongst colourful items lost was

79

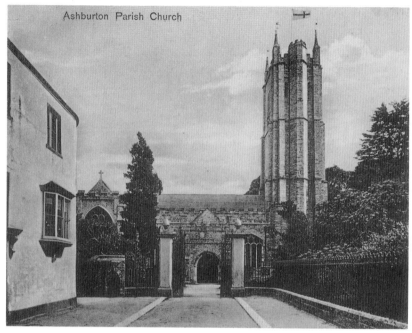

Ashburton Parish Church

ASHBURTON ... The parish church.

a memorial to a local woman, Elizabeth Ireland, who died in 1779:
'Here I lie at the chancel door;
Here I lie because I'm poor;
The further in the more you pay
Here I lie as warm as they'.

If it was truly a case that 'the further in the more you pay', then the relatives of John Dunning, who was to die as the first Lord Ashburton, would have had to pay a considerable price to have been commemorated in a prime position behind the organ. Wealthy? Yes; successful? Yes; modest? Well, perhaps. John Dunning is recalled as a man who *'by his private virtues, united with the exertion of rare and excellent talents to that pre-eminence, which neither birth nor titles can bestow'.*

At least Elizabeth Ireland's relatives showed humility!

In the churchyard is the grave of a French officer, Francois Guidon, Lieutenant of the French 46th Regiment of the Line.

How could Francois, a native of Cambrai, have come to rest in a plot of Devon earth?

He was one of the French prisoners-of-war held at Princetown in the early 1800s. It was customary that, provided they undertook not to try to escape, French officers could be quartered in civilian accommodation within a reasonable distance of the prison. They were even paid a subsistence allowance towards their living costs.

By the time the railway reached Ashburton, in 1872, with the extension of the existing Buckfastleigh, Totnes and South Devon Railway network, Asburton was in decline in terms of prosperity, industry, and population. Those who still worked in the wool trade had started to travel to other areas for employment. Had the directors of the South Devon Railway not by-passed the town twenty-six years earlier, there might have been a slim hope of survival. As Dr W G Hoskins wrote in *Devon*: '*The arrival in 1872 of a branch railway from Totnes – one of the most picturesque little railways in England – did nothing to revive the dying town; and it mouldered gently*

East St. Ashburton.

EAST STREET ... This postcard, the original in soft colours, was produced by a Dawlish publisher.

81

on into the twentieth-century, losing its young people to places like Torquay and Newton Abbot, and attracting only the elderly, looking for peace and quiet and reasonably cheap living'.

Mourning the passing of such towns, Dr Hoskins paints an eloquent pen picture of: 'these silent little places with their peeling plaster, where cats bask on sunlit window-sills and prostrate dogs hardly bother to stir as an occasional car makes a detour around them in the road; the silence of a summer afternoon broken only at vast intervals by the short pang-pang of the church clock; the sun on the blinds of the draper's shop, the wasps crawling wearily over the dried-up buns in the bakery and the sticky jars of sweets. No more three-day fairs, no more brisk markets every week for corn and cattle, sheep and provisions; no more cloth merchants and weavers, no more tin-miners and copper-miners; no more masons and quarrymen, ostlers and coachmen; no more the ring of smithies up and down the street, the great stamping horses and the glossy cattle; but only the dusky black cats, the comatose dogs, and the eternal wasps'.

Lest the bakers and confectioners of today's Ashburton read this, it should be stressed that Dr Hoskins was writing in 1954.

PRINCETOWN ... The grim prison where so many French soldiers were held in the 19th century.

Fingle, Fingall, Fingill ... or just Beautiful

F ar be it from a humble author to step into a minefield of controversy, but is Fingle Bridge really Fingle Bridge at all? Let no less an authority than the Rev Samuel Rowe explain in simple, non-technical terms: *'Some topographers, misled by sound, or anxious to import an Ossianic character to the spot, have spelt this word "Fingall". Mr Short derives Fingle from Fyn, Cornish, a boundary, and Gelli, hazel. May not Gill, the well-known designation of a water-fall among the Cambrian Celts, form part of the original word which would then be Fingill? Fingill would mean the White Waterfall'*, he points out with commendable logic and simplicity!

We must all be obliged to the Reverend gentleman for that earth-shattering disclosure.

Whatever its true name, there is no denying that Fingle Bridge is a place of spectacular beauty in an area of renowned beauty spots. Crossing the Teign, near Drewsteignton, it is the site of a granite bridge dating back some three or four hundred years. Few places demand such a steep and dramatic upward sweep of the eyes towards higher ground.

And the tea house?

It was set up to cater for the growing number of tourists who were being increasingly attracted to Dartmoor's charms in the 1880s and 1890s. No doubt water for drinks was discreetly drawn from the stream. In an obvious attempt to try to make a structure of posts and galvanised iron look really rustic, the owners of the tea house tried to disguise the impact of modern materials with a gentle artificial roof of brushwood and bracken in a landscaped and environmentally-friendly way.

Despite the obvious changes in tastes, Devon cream teas were

FINGLE BRIDGE TEA SHELTER 10513

already very much in evidence and a feature of shrewd local marketing as 'traditional Devonshire fare'. Although many tourists came from quite far afield, to be accommodated in farmhouses, cottages and guest-houses, there was a growing trade in day-trippers from Exeter and Torbay. Some small towns had an official guide who would drive a courtesy coach, even a pony and trap, to the nearest railway station to give tourists a taste of the Moors.

Peter Tavy and Mary Tavy – and How They Were Called as Witnesses Before a Stupid Judge

ONLY an idiot or a hero, it was once said, would dare to mention Mary Tavy and Peter Tavy in the same breath. It was argued that they might share a name, but that was as far as it need go.

Whether or not successive Bishops of Exeter were fools or brave men is an unwise line to pursue. In any case, they added to the points of division by referring to the respective churches, St Peter Tavy and St Mary the Virgin, Mary Tavy.

There can, however, be no doubting the ignorant folly of the judge at Exeter Assizes who confused the addresses of two witnesses with their names, and called for Peter and Mary Tavy to enter the witness box. When they failed to respond, he ordered the doors of the court to be closed *'in order that Peter and Mary do not depart without the leave of this court without charge of contempt'*.

It has also been said that, like brother and sister, the two Tavys do not always exist in family harmony.

Asked which Tavy was which, a wise neutral observer said: *'One has the beauty: the other, the people'*. He declined to differentiate further!

Peter Tavy church was built around 1500 but, according to one expert, was 'abominably restored'. This contradicts the view of William Crossing, in 1909 that Peter Tavy is: *'a quiet little place, with a church embossed in trees, a chapel, a school and a small inn'*.

Its gentle churchyard contains many tombstones ranging, both in quality and in the richness of prose, from the poor to the pompous, and from the polished to the poignant.

Of these, the memorial to the five children of a former vicar, Richard Eveleigh, carries sadness and a strange but peaceful

PLACE OF WORSHIP … Peter Tavy Church.

inevitability stemming, as it did, from the 1630s when none but the super-fit stood any chance of survival.

In just over five years, Richard and his wife followed five tiny coffins to the graveside to bury two Maries, two Elizabeths and one Eleanor. All five little girls died before their second birthday and the tablet to their memory is larger than the soil they occupy.

Destined to perpetual memory, the inscription reads:

Under this stone by nature's fatall doome
Five sisters lie cropt in their tender bloome
They breathed awhile and looked the world about
And like new lighted candles soon went out
Their sunne no sooner did arise, but set,
Their journies' end at setting forth they met.
They op'd their eyes, and in the world's disdaine
Full quickly did they close them up againe.
Their life was short, the less they did amisse,
The shorter life the longer is their blisse.
Five infant sisters from one wombe,
Here lie together in one tombe:
Their tide did ebb before full sea,
Their welcome was their well away.
Their parents have no cause to weepe,
Sith they lie here, but in a sleepe.'

To Mary Tavy came John Taylor, one of Britain's great mining engineers. At the end of the eighteenth century he became, at the age of only 19, manager of the Wheal Friendship mine. Realising that adequate supplies of water were the lifeblood of the industry (as well as, potentially, the element that could drown a mine and the men in it), he designed and built a stone aqueduct and leat to serve Wheal Friendship.

Taylor, who came from an old-established Norwich family, had trained in land-surveying and civil engineering. He was destined to become world-renowned in the widest circles of metalliferous mining at home and abroad.

So advanced was the engineering brilliance of Taylor's work that, in 1803 – when he was still only 26 – he was engaged to link Tavistock to the Tamar at Morwellham by a short canal.

The actual length of the canal, about four miles, might make the

REMEMBERED ...
The Rev Samuel Rowe
and below, William Crossing's
grave at Mary Tavy.

task seem deceptively simple. It was not and the project took some fourteen years to complete.

There was no disputing the need. Morwellham, a river port, could be reached by incoming consignments of coal and lime for the mines and quarries and carried on seagoing vessels which, having discharged their cargo, could then re-load with locally-produced mineral ores and stone and slate.

The only problem was that of geography in that a huge hill and dramatic land contours stood in the way.

Even under John Taylor's inspired leadership, fourteen years were to pass between approval being given for the work to begin and the official opening of the Tavistock canal on 24 June 1817.

In that time, a two-mile tunnel had been dug under Morwell Down, and a double-lined inclined plane built to carry the ore-bearing vehicles some 80 metres down to the quayside.

The work was, in the main, forced labour by French prisoners-of-war.

The canal barges were loaded on to trolleys which ran down the grooved rails of the inclined plane, the rate of climb and descent controlled by windlass and chain.

While John Taylor wrestled with the problems of the canal, another Tavistock engineer – John Thomas – created and perfected a steam carriage *'adapted for travelling on turnpike roads, and having a condensing apparatus which prevents the emission of steam, and reduces the consumption of both coal and water'*.

The money generated by the work and genius of John Taylor and John Thomas played an important part in creating the prosperity that would, eventually, pay for the rebuilding of the centre of Tavistock.

Perhaps the greatest compliment to Mary Tavy is that it was the chosen resting place of that great observer and lover of Dartmoor, William Crossing. His great work, *One Hundred Years on Dartmoor* suggests no favoured spot other than in, perhaps, the following words: *'The observer, from a border eminence commanding a far-reaching view of the Moor, sees before him a vast sweep of dusky, rolling hills, with here and there a tor peeping over some dark ridge, or cresting some granite-strewn height. Cattle, and sheep, and ponies of the Dartmoor breed browse upon the sides of the hills and in the valleys, but beyond these scarce a sign of life is visible. Few sounds break the stillness, the chief being the cry of the curlew, or the falling waters of some near-by stream. A sense of loneliness possesses the beholder, and he feels he is looking down a scene from which "man is far away", and which the ages have done little to alter.'*

Dare any man deny that Crossing was describing the area beyond Mary Tavy and stretching towards Lydford?

Peter Tavy shares with Whitchurch the facility of having a pub literally at the bottom of the church garden, but it is doubtful if many vicars faced with the same logistics of spiritual and temporal supply amongst virtually the same consumers would have taken similar steps to those of one of Peter Tavy's vicars, the Rev McBean.

Faced with the problem of divided loyalty attendance brought about by the coincidence of respective hours of service in the church and the pub, he would never start his sermon until he had been assured that the pub was empty and that the church was as full as might reasonably be expected.

Rather than leave the matter to fate, divine intervention – or even the freedom of the people to choose – he would despatch his churchwarden to check that the public bars were empty while the congregation were singing the hymn before his address.

Such a task would fully test the diplomacy of any mere mortal – but, for the churchwarden, things were even more delicate as he was a relation of the publican.

He was indeed on the horns of a dilemma. Should he disregard his loyalty to the cloth and turn a blind eye to customers lurking in the snug? Or should he urge them to come to church, thereby incurring family wrath?

He solved the problem in a most intelligent and faultless way.

Approaching the bar windows, he would circle the inn a couple of times saying loudly that he was on the way … and allowing the imbibers time to be out of sight by the time he entered the bar.

He was then able to report back – truthfully – that the bar was empty when he entered it.

The vicar, thus reassured, could then begin his sermon in the knowledge that drink had attracted no absentees from the power (and length) of his oratory.

How Jim Perrott's Great Idea Succeeded, but Posed an Undreamed-of Problem

CRANMERE Pool isn't a pool at all, really. At one time it probably was, but nowadays its colourful name is one of the worst mis-descriptions of modern Dartmoor, for the so-called 'pool' is just a wide expanse of bog.

Even the Rev Samuel Rowe, publicist extraordinaire of the delights of Dartmoor, ran out of glowing adjectives when, in the 1840s, he wrote that it would be wise to abandon any form of transport other than two very reliable feet for the final approach to Cranmere – lying, as it does, in *'the vast expanse of boggy tableland, which characterizes the remotest and inaccessible parts of the moorland wilderness'*.

The journey, he warned. *'is toilsome, as you are continually plunging into the plashy soil; or, to avoid getting knee-deep in the bogs, are constrained to leap from tuft to tuft of the firmer patches of rushy ground. Nor is there anything in the surrounding scenery to cheer the wanderer who requires a succession of new and attractive objects to animate him in his progress. Here the image of "a waste and howling wilderness" is fully realised ... this is one of the few spots where no indication of man's presence or occupancy are to be traced'*.

Within a couple of years the reverend gentleman was to be proved wrong – but of that, more later.

Cranmere Pool undoubtedly was once a proper pool of deep, clear water, its saucer-like bowl holding the fruits of snow and winter rain until well into the parched days of summer. A few years before Samuel Rowe, another clergyman, the Rev Shaw, walked in search of it but found *'no pool at all, but just a small piece of bare black bog. The large bog itself is of interest as the source of many rivers; but there is absolutely no interest in Cranmere Pool which is nothing but a snare and delusion for tourists'.*

But what turned a pool, once basking in romantic vision, into a bare black bog of virtually no appeal whatsoever?

Enter some waterlogged cattle and sheep; a thirsty population; and an anonymous – but significant – terrier.

These three unlikely partners have variously been blamed for what happened to the pool in the early 1800s.

Something undoubtedly occurred that caused man to interfere with the water containment of nature. Some authorities argue that so many sheep and cattle were drowned in the deep waters of the pool that it had to be drained. Others suggest that, as summers grew long and hotter and as communities grew, it was decided to divert the water into the public supply via one of the many neighbouring rivers having their source nearby.

But what of the little dog?

He, it seems, was carried away while pursuing a wily fox. Reynard went to ground at Cranmere and the dog – showing perseverance rather than intelligence – followed it into an ambush underground. As its frantic owners dug to free it, they accidentally obstructed the flow of water which, once diverted, never returned to its original levels, turning the pool into a bog.

But let us return to the views of the two clergymen – Samuel Rowe and his *'where no indication of man's presence or occupancy are to be traced'*, and his fellow cleric's bald statement that *'there is absolutely no interest in Cranmere Pool which is nothing but a snare and a delusion for tourists'.*

Enter Jim Perrott, of Chagford.

With the worthy books of Shaw and Rowe already in the lists of Dartmoor best-sellers, James Perrott was equally renowned as a tourist guide. He'd been born in 1815 – the year of Waterloo – and grew up in an era in which communications were, to say the least, not of the speediest.

When George III died in 1820, in London, the news took some eight weeks to reach the tiny Dartmoor village of Bridford.

Although the Royal Mail might carry a letter from Plymouth or Exeter to Okehampton or Tavistock in a matter of hours, it could be days – if not weeks – before someone from the intended recipient's village spotted it in the post office window and carried it for

CRANMERE POOL ... 'A bare black bog.'

its last few miles to its destination.

It was against this background that Jim Perrott introduced what was to become the network of Dartmoor letterboxes which, by the 1970s, had become so wide that it seemed that they would have to be banned in the interests of conservation.

Perrott found that, despite the dismal writings of the two clergymen, increasing numbers of people visiting Dartmoor wished to go to Cranmere Pool. And, human nature being what it is, they wanted to boast about their success in beating a particularly difficult set of physical hazards in order to get there.

In 1854, therefore, he found a convenient hole in a hedge at Cranmere Pool and carefully placed a bottle in it so that visitors could leave their calling cards to prove they had visited the site.

The bottle was soon full. It was replaced by a tin box carefully protected by a little heap of stones.

Some fifty years later, as calling cards were losing their popularity, and capacity was becoming limited, a visitor's book was provided. In 1905 it attracted 609 signatures. By 1908, the numbers signing had multiplied threefold ... and Jim Perrott's idea had progressed from bottle in hedge, to tin in stone mound and onwards to granite pillar containing cupboard, book and post-box.

In 1894 a second box was provided, this time at Belstone Tor and, in 1939, a third was placed in position at Duck's Pool.

By then a great ritual had become self-perpetuating. Walkers, in addition to signing the visitors' book, would frank their own souvenirs with the rubber stamp identifying the letterbox. Additionally, they would leave a self-addressed (and stamped!) postcard in the box, duly franked with the identifying mark, with the request that the next walker should post it from their home town upon their return.

It was an idea that became a custom and, ultimately, a tradition that was rarely violated.

However, it was an idea which – after a very slow gestation – was to accelerate in the 1960s and 1970s to such a degree that there were serious thoughts of curbing the network.

Walkers, fired with the innocent pleasures of having been seen to conquer the walks to the boxes, began to place receptacles all over the place. These – often tins or old ammunition cases – were frequently unsightly and painted in vivid colours. Not only were they placed in age-old hedges, but were sometimes marked by unattractive and crudely-painted signs and finger posts. The craze to sign-in at as many points as possible caused the insensitive to trample through antiquities; clamber over fragile stoneworks; and even ravage walls and windbreaks in search of them.

As the total of 'boxes' (sometimes merely ice cream tubs or cigarette boxes, but each containing its identifying rubber stamp) soared to the 500 mark – and beyond – the Dartmoor National Park authority warned that the idea had run riot and was beginning to pose a threat. There was indeed even talk of a strict system of registration in a bid to outlaw unofficial boxes.

The threat had its effect and the spread was halted to a containable number.

Books and Sources Consulted

Baring-Gould, Rev Sabine, *A BOOK OF DARTMOOR*, Bodley Head;
Bradford-Barton, D B, *COPPER MINING IN DEVON & CORNWALL*,
  Truro Bookshop;
Burton, S H, *DEVON VILLAGES*, Robert Hale;
CHAMBERS BIOGRAPHICAL DICTIONARY, W. & R. Chambers;
Crossing, William, *ONE HUNDRED YEARS ON DARTMOOR*,
  Western Morning News;
Gunnell, Clive, *TO TAVISTOCK GOOSIE FAIR*, Bossiney Books;
Hoskins, Dr W G, *DEVON*, Collins;
Lewis, G R, *THE STANNARIES*, D. Bradford-Barton;
Murray, John, *MURRAY'S HANDBOOK FOR DEVON AND CORNWALL,
  1859*, David & Charles;
THE NEW STANDARD ENCYCLOPAEDIA, Odhams Press;
Norway, Arthur H, *HIGHWAYS & BYWAYS IN DEVON AND CORNWALL*,
  MacMillan & Co;
Pearse-Chope, R, *EARLY TOURS IN DEVON & CORNWALL*,
  David & Charles;
Penny, A D V, *KELLY COLLEGE REGISTER 1877-1927*,
  Tavistock Printing Co.;
Pettit, Paul, *SHELL GUIDE TO DEVON, CORNWALL & THE ISLES OF
  SCILLY*, Michael Joseph;
Rowe, Rev. Samuel A, *A PERAMBULATION OF DEVON*, Devon Books;
TAVISTOCK GAZETTE;
TAVISTOCK TIMES;
Thomas, David St John, *REGIONAL HISTORY OF THE RAILWAYS OF
  GREAT BRITAIN*, Phoenix House;
Smith, Vian, *PORTRAIT OF DARTMOOR*, Robert Hale;
Ward Lock, *DARTMOOR, 1929-30*, Ward Lock;
WESTERN MORNING NEWS;
White, William, *HISTORY, GAZETTEER AND DIRECTORY OF DEVON*,
  David & Charles;
Woodcock, G, *TAVISTOCK'S YESTERDAYS*, G. Woodcock.

More Bossiney Books ...

DARTMOOR REFLECTIONS
by David Mudd
'... an engaging mix of fact and folklore that blends together in a most enjoyable and enlightening read.'
Roger Malone, Tavistock Times
'... a valuable addition to Dartmoor literature.' June Glover, South Hams Group of Newspapers

THE CRUEL CORNISH SEA
by David Mudd

MYSTERIES OF THE SOUTH WEST
by Tamsin Thomas of BBC Radio Cornwall
A tour of ancient sites in Cornwall and on Dartmoor.
'There is little doubt that Tamsin Thomas has become the 'Voice of Cornwall'.
Ronnie Hoyle, North Cornwall Advertiser

AROUND AND ABOUT THE FAL
by David Mudd
A rich tapestry of a famous Cornish river and its people.

DEVON REFLECTIONS
by Jilly Carter
In her years with TSW, Jilly Carter travelled thousands of miles for news stories and interviews. She now uses that knowledge – and affection for Devon – in producing a balanced portrait of the county.

SUPERNATURAL INVESTIGATION
by Michael Williams
'... has to be the one you read in front of a roaring fire, curtains closed against the howling gale and a stiff whisky within arm's reach to calm the nerves.' Wendy Hanwell, Tavistock Times

GHOSTS OF DEVON
by Peter Underwood, 44 photographs and drawings.
Peter Underwood, President of the Ghost Club, writes of the ghostly stories that saturate the County of Devon, a land full of mystery and of ghostly lore and legend.
'Packed with photographs, this is a fascinating book.' Herald Express

STRANGE STORIES FROM DEVON
by Rosemary Anne Lauder and Michael Williams. 46 photographs.
Strange shapes and places – strange characters – the man they couldn't hang, and a Salcombe mystery, the Lynmouth disaster and a mysterious house are only some of the strange stories.
'A riveting read.' The Plymouth Times

LEGENDS OF DEVON
by Sally Jones. 60 photographs and drawings.
Devon is a mine of folklore and myth. Here in a journey through legendary Devon, Sally Jones brings into focus some fascinating tales, showing us that the line dividing fact and legend is an intriguing one.
'...Sally Jones has trodden the path of legendary Devon well ...' Tavistock Times

We shall be delighted to send you our catalogue giving full details of our growing list of titles and forthcoming publications. If you have difficulty in obtaining our titles, write direct to Bossiney Books, Land's End, St Teath, Bodmin, Cornwall.